This Cat is Photoshopped

The Book

By Tara Richter

RICHTER® PUBLISHING

Published by Richter Publishing LLC www.richterpublishing.com

Book Cover Design: Tara Richter

Illustrations by Tara Richter

978-1-954094-28-4 Paperback

DISCLAIMER

This book is designed to provide information on photoshopped cats. This information is provided and sold for entertainment purposes only and the publisher and author do not offer any legal or medical advice. In the case of a need for any such expertise, consult with the appropriate professional. This book does not contain all information available on the subject. This book has not been created to be specific to any individual people or organization's situation or needs. Reasonable efforts have been made to make this book as accurate as possible. However, there may be typographical and or content errors. Therefore, this book should serve only as a general guide. This book contains information that might be dated or erroneous and is intended only to educate and entertain. The author and publisher shall have no liability or responsibility to any person or entity regarding any loss or damage incurred, or alleged to have incurred, directly or indirectly, by the information contained in this book or as a result of anyone acting or failing to act upon the information in this book. You hereby agree never to sue and to hold the author and publisher harmless from any and all claims arising out of the information contained in this book. You hereby agree to be bound by this disclaimer, covenant not to sue and release. You may return this book within the guaranteed time period for a full refund. All characters appearing in this work are for fun only. Some names, places and inconsequential facts were adjusted to protect privacy. Any resemblance to other real persons, living or dead, is purely coincidental. The opinions and stories in this book are the views of the authors and not those of the publisher.

Table of Contents

Introduction

The cat photoshops in this book have mostly been done from my iPhone in free apps. I do have a degree in Graphic Design, skilled in Photoshop, but the intent was never to make this fine artwork. Some shops are bad, quick and all are super cheesy. So cheesy. I stumbled across this group on Facebook awhile ago of cat lovers who make funny photoshops of their pets. A cat mom or dad will volunteer a photo of their fur baby and let us designers have a go at it. Sorry kitties, it's all their fault what happened to you. So to the art critics out there, this was all for fun. A five minute quick edit on an app on my phone. And viola a hilarious image of your favorite feline to share on social media. My intent was never to publish them, but while I was backing up my laptop I realized I had hundreds of these little gems! Well I couldn't *not* let these go to waste. I had to share them with the world!

In October of 2021 Callie, my crazy Calico cat passed away from cancer. This group was one of the bright spots in my day. It is literally the only group on social media where there is no fighting, no politics, no nonsense just happy people sharing their feline friends. It makes me literally laugh out loud every time I look at the group and warms my heart to see other crazy cats living their best lives.

So have fun and I hope you enjoy these photoshops as much as I did creating them. They are all my shops besides the dedication page that the admin of the FB group did, Helen Yang, which I greatly appreciate. For the famous people appearing in this book, I hope everyone knows this is all for fun, don't be a Karen. All proceeds coming from the sales of this book, I am donating back to a shelter or non-profit to help save kitties and find them forever homes. Adopt today.

Sincerely,
Tara Richter

Helen Yang

I dedicate this book to my crazy Calico cat Callie. I miss you so much. You gave everyone hell. And I still have scars to prove it. I hope you're giving everyone up there a run for their money.
Love You Poopers

IT IS TIME TO GO.

Was I a Good Cat?

NO.

I'M TOLD YOU WERE THE BEST.

seebangnow

Demon Cats

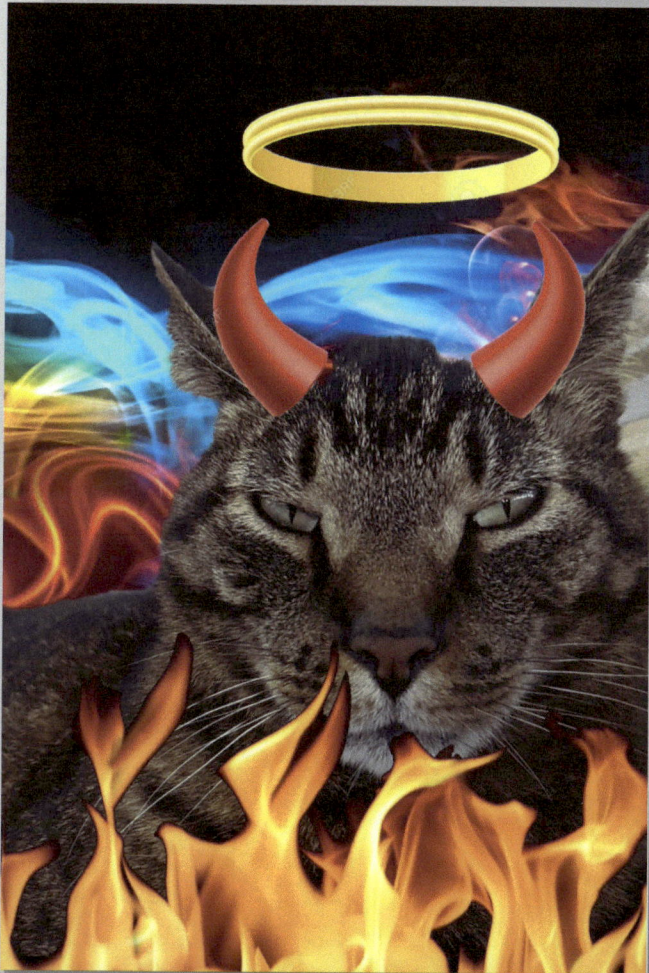

Drunk and or Under the Influence Cats

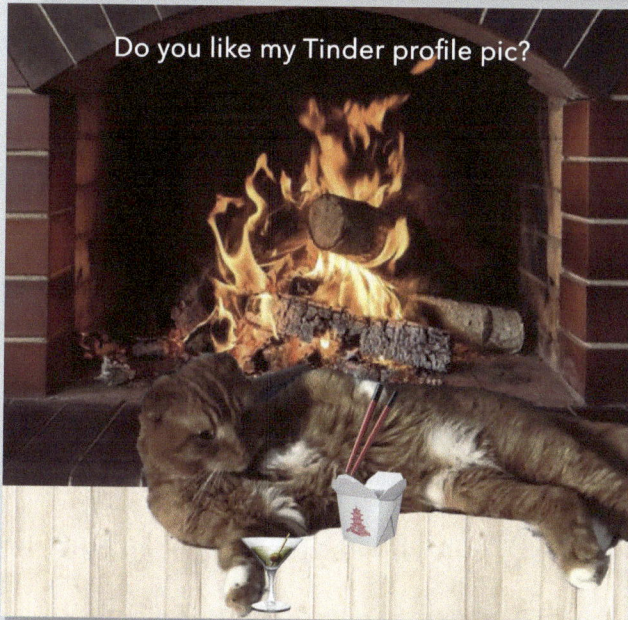

Do you like my Tinder profile pic?

I need more wine! Why are the pours here so small ?!

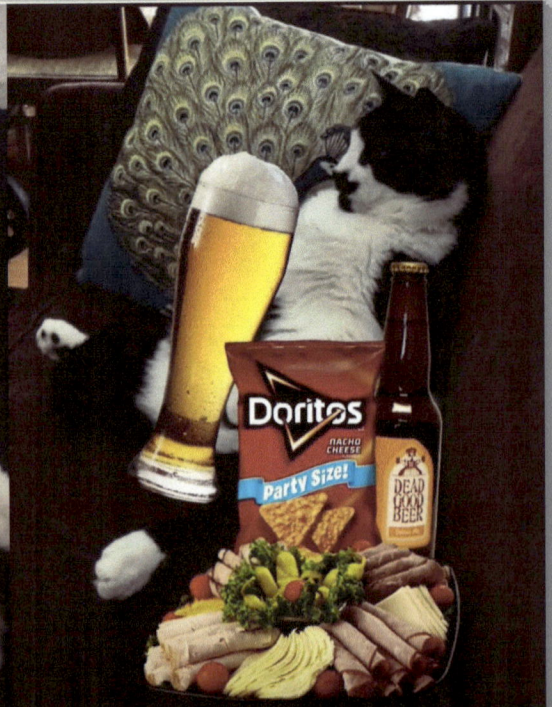

Do You Like My Tinder Profile Pic?

Foodie Cats

I SEE DEAD PEOPLE.

THERE IS A GLITCH IN THE MATRIX

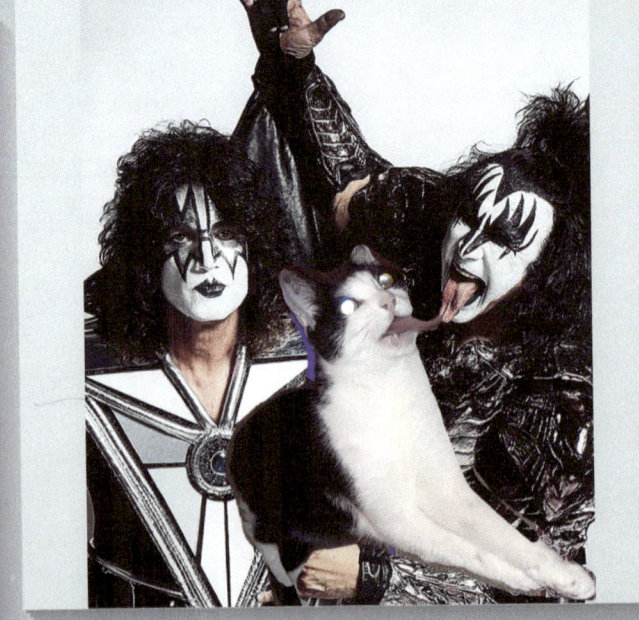

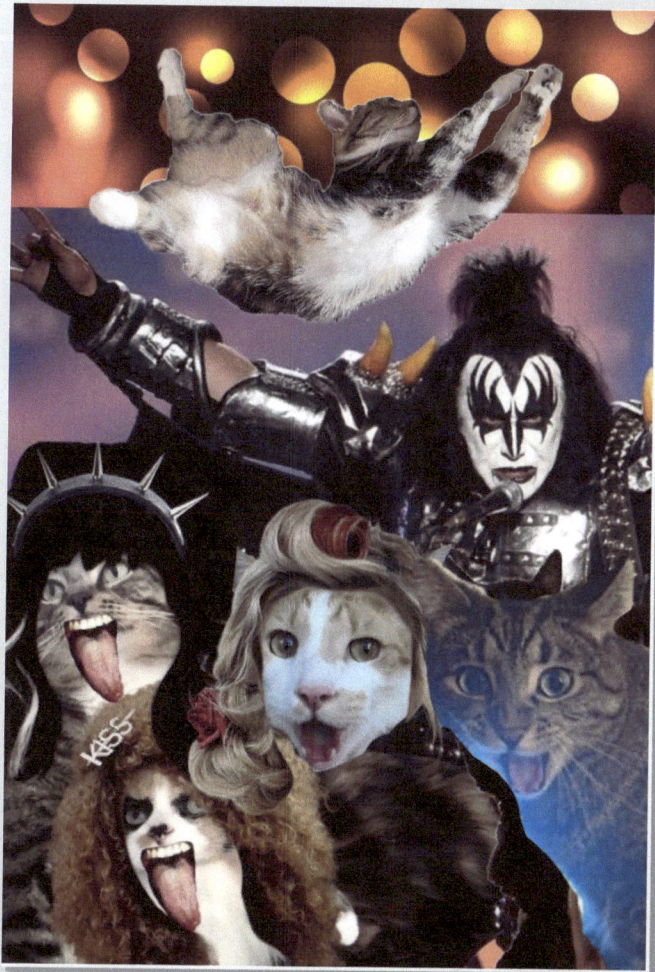

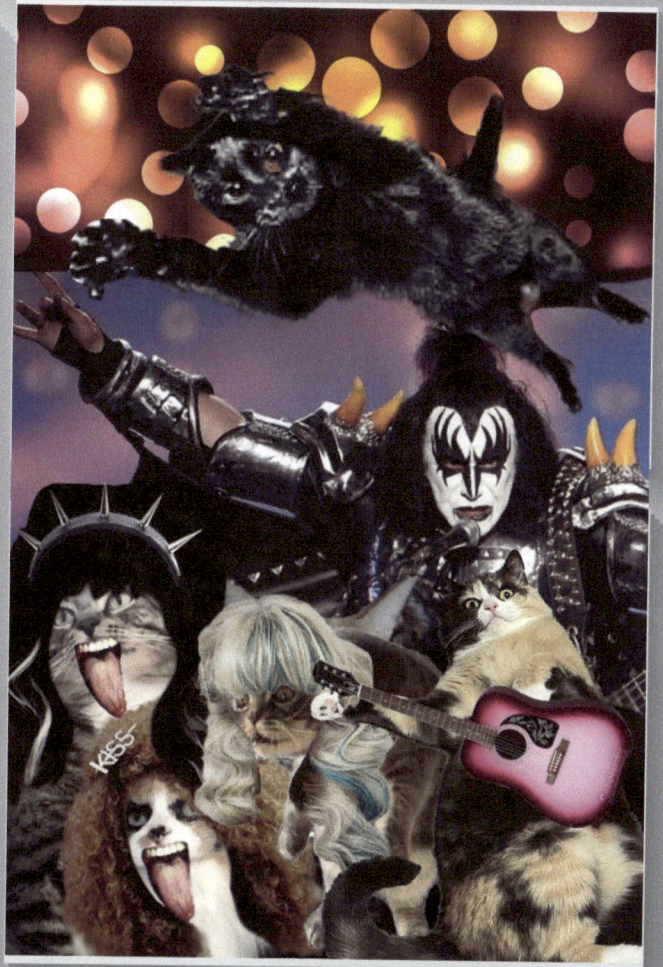

NATURE
CATS

Nobody:
Jim:

Don't act like you're not impressed."

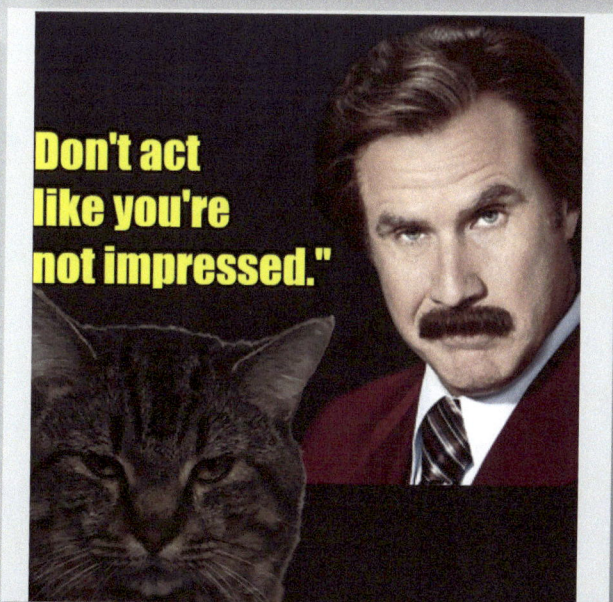

Paint me like one of your french girls.

About the Author

Tara Richter is the President of Richter Publishing LLC. She specializes in helping business owners how to write their non-fiction story in 4 weeks & publish a book in order to become an expert in their industry. She has been featured on CNN, ABC, Daytime TV, FOX, SSN, Channel 10 News, USA TODAY, Beverly Hills Times and radio stations all over the world.

Her degree is in Graphic Design and she worked in the copy and print industry in the Silicon Valley. She has written and published 15 of her own books in just a few short years that have become #1 Amazon Best Sellers and won other awards. Tara now has published many other authors all over the world including Anthony Amos & celebrity entrepreneur, Kevin Harrington, Shark from ABC's "Shark Tank" with their joint book, "How to Catch a Shark." She has also worked with many doctors, lawyers, non-profits and Fortune 500 Corporations such as Blooming Inc. Tara was juried into an art gallery in downtown St. Petersburg when she was 28 years old featuring her artwork at the Artists Gallery Royale. She was the youngest artist in the gallery by 20 some years featuring her Photoshop skills back between 2004-2005.

We kept trying to find a picture of the author, but we only found Callie in her office instead. In her chair, laying on her computer, sleeping on her keyboard. Not sure what happened to the human. But you can find her other books on Amazon here: http://www.amazon.com/Tara-Richter/e/B00CGKD8FG or go to her website: www.richterpublishing.com

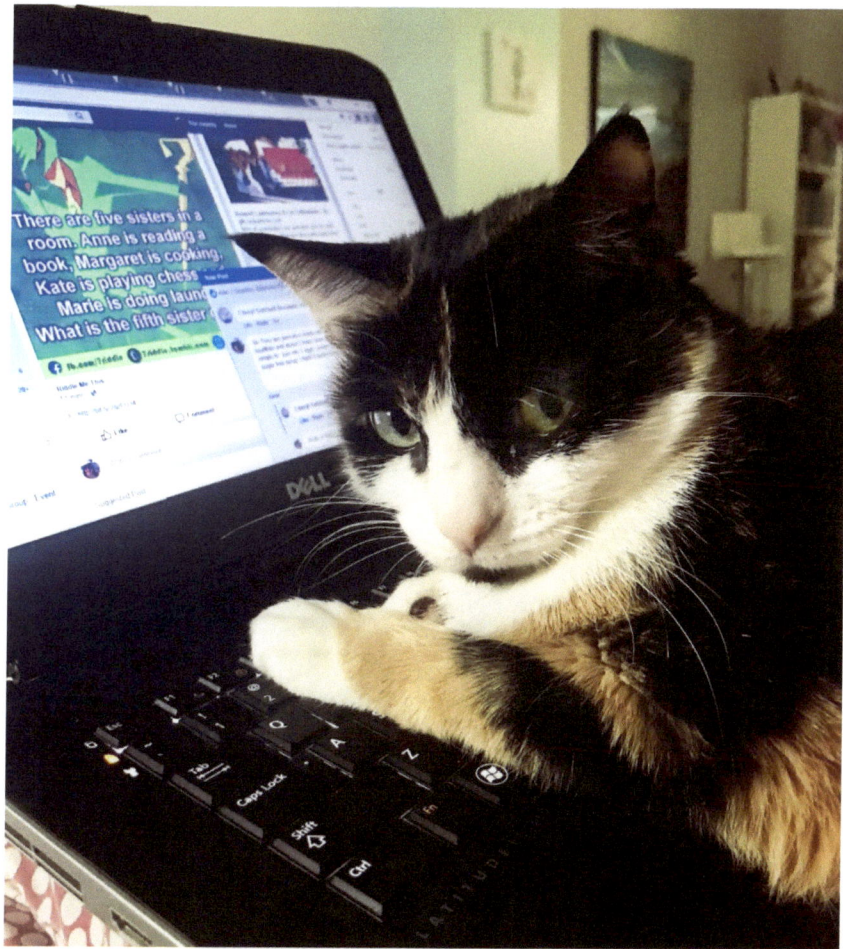

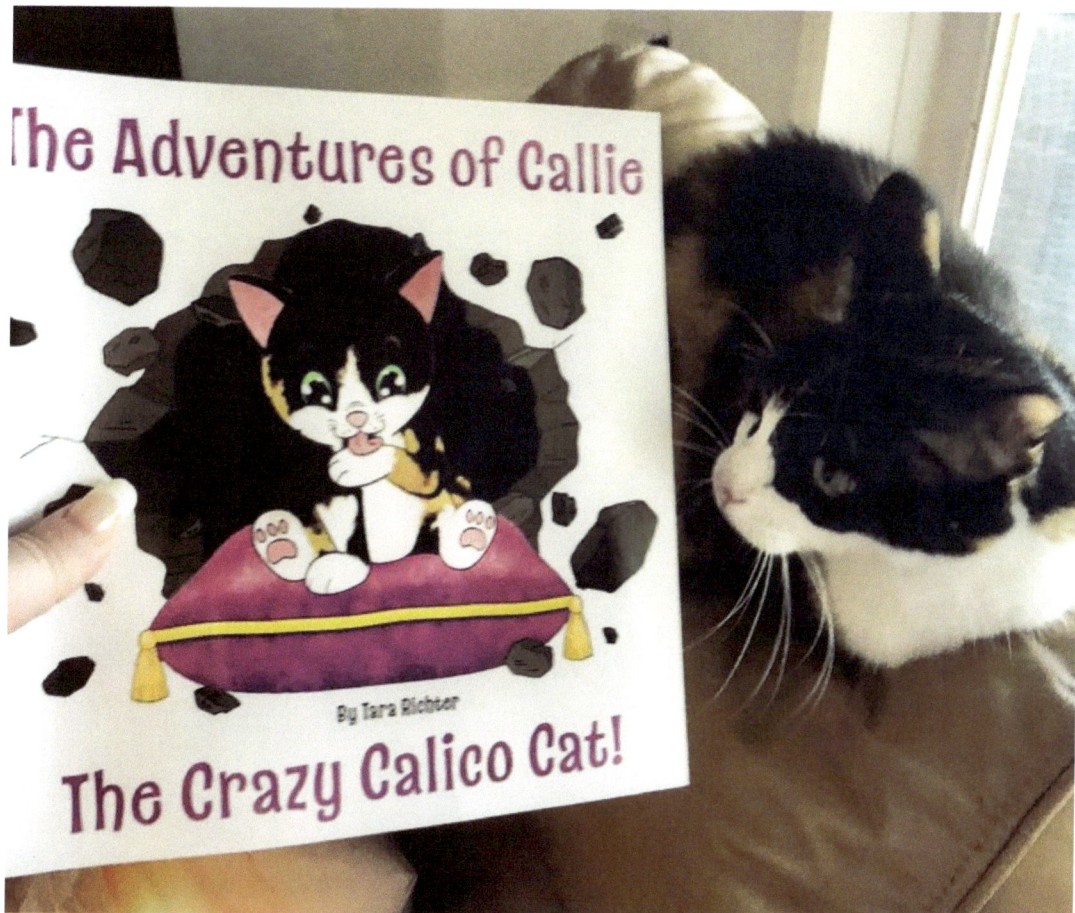

The Adventures of Callie

By Tara Richter

The Crazy Calico Cat!